word building

At the Party

Word Building with Prefixes and Suffixes

Pam Scheunemann

Consulting Editor, Diane Craig, M.A./Reading Specialist

A Division of ABDO

ABDO
Publishing Company

Printed in the United States of America, North Mankato, Minnesota
062012
092012

PRINTED ON RECYCLED PAPER

Editor: Liz Salzmann
Content Developer: Nancy Tuminelly
Interior Design: Kelly Doudna, Mighty Media, Inc.
Production: Oona Gaarder-Juntti, Mighty Media, Inc.
Photo Credits: BananaStock Brand X Pictures, Comstock Images, David Sacks, George Doyle, Hermera Technologies, IT Stock Free, Jochen Sand, Jupiterimages, Kraig Scarbinsky, Maria Teijeiro, Polka Dot images, Shutterstock, Stockbyte, Thinkstock Images, Thomas Northcut

Library of Congress Cataloging-in-Publication Data
Scheunemann, Pam, 1955-
 At the party : word building with prefixes and suffixes / Pam Scheunemann.
   p. cm. -- (Word building)
 ISBN 978-1-61714-968-9
 1. English language--Suffixes and prefixes--Juvenile literature. 2. Vocabulary--Juvenile literature. 3. Language arts (Elementary) I. Title.
 PE1175.S326 2012
 428.1--dc22
                        2010054485

Super SandCastle™ books are created by a team of professional educators, reading specialists, and content developers around five essential components—phonemic awareness, phonics, vocabulary, text comprehension, and fluency—to assist young readers as they develop reading skills and strategies and increase their general knowledge. All books are written, reviewed, and leveled for guided reading, early reading intervention, and Accelerated Reader® programs for use in shared, guided, and independent reading and writing activities to support a balanced approach to literacy instruction.

contents

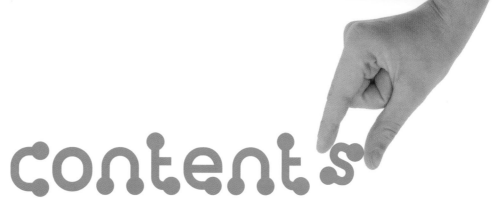

what is word Building?

Word building is adding groups of letters to a word. The added letters change the word's meaning.

joy s

Prefix

Some groups of letters are added to the beginning of words. They are called prefixes. Some prefixes have more than one meaning.

Suffix

Some groups of letters are added to the end of words. They are called suffixes. Some suffixes have more than one meaning.

en + joy + ing

prefix + base word + suffix

enjoying

The prefix **en** means to cause to be.
The base word **joy** means happiness.
The suffix **ing** means that the action is happening now.
Enjoying means something is causing happiness now.

Let's Build words

call

Ron calls his friend, Matt. He invites Matt to a party.

Shelly is calling her friend Emily. She says she can come to Emily's party.

Tonya gets a phone call.
The caller is her grandmother.

calls

The suffix **s** means that the action is happening now.

calling

The suffix **ing** means that the action is happening now.

caller

The suffix **er** means the person or thing that does the action.

More Words

called, recall, recalls, recaller, recalled, recalling, recallable

take

Jacob and Pam take pictures with their phone.

Sara retakes the picture.

Debbie is taking a picture.

retakes

The prefix **re** means to do it again.

The suffix **s** means that the action is happening now.

taking

The suffix **ing** means that the action is happening now.

More Words

taker, taken, retake, retaken, retaking

open

Amy rips open the red envelope.

Walter brings unopened presents to the party.

Monica has fun opening
her presents.

unopened

The prefix **un** means not
or opposite.

The suffix **ed** turns a word
into an adjective.

opening

The suffix **ing** means that
the action is happening now.

More Words

opens, opened, opener,
openings, unopen, reopen,
reopens, reopened, reopening

happy

Erin wishes her grandma a happy birthday.

Raina is unhappy that her friends are late.

Zach is happiest when he can play outside.

unhappy

The prefix **un** means not or opposite.

happiest

The suffix **est** means most.

More Words

happier, happily, happiness, unhappiness, unhappiest

ᖇ᙭ Rule ᖇ᙭

When a word ends with *y*, change the *y* to *i* before adding **est**.

thank

Diane's mom hugs her to thank her for the flowers.

Gabby is not thankful for her beautiful gift.

thankfulness

The suffix **ful** means full of.

The suffix **ness** turns an adjective into a noun.

More Words

thanks, thanked, thanking, thankless, thanklessness

Eddy's family shows their thankfulness for their meal.

Marty Enjoyed the Party!

HELLO
my name is
Kyle

Marty enjoys parties of every style.
He finds it most enjoyable when
he goes with Kyle.
Marty and Kyle are welcome
everywhere they go.
Unwelcome is a word that
they do not know!

HELLO
my name is
Marty

At one party, Marty
was acting weird.
He acted like a cat and
everybody cheered.
When Kyle played his
music, they danced and
tapped their feet.
Then they saw Marty tapping
his tail to the beat!

Everybody liked to see Marty.

He was the unlikely star of the party!

And when the party was over,

Kyle stayed to help clean.

Even Marty helped out.

He was a cleaning machine!

HELLO
my name is
Marty

match it up!

Choose the word with the correct prefix or suffix to complete each sentence.

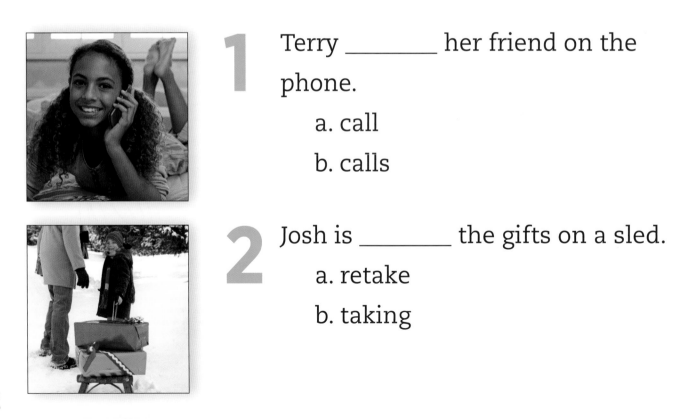

1 Terry _____ her friend on the phone.

    a. call

    b. calls

2 Josh is _____ the gifts on a sled.

    a. retake

    b. taking

3 Hannah's gifts are _____.

    a. opens

    b. unopened

4 Mary sprays window _____ on the window.

    a. cleaner

    b. cleaned

5 Dogs are _____ at the park.

    a. unwelcome

    b. welcoming

Glossary

adjective (pp. 11, 15) – a word used to describe someone or something. Tall, green, round, happy, and cold are all adjectives.

cheer (p. 18) – to shout because you are happy about something.

envelope (p. 10) – a paper container for something flat, such as a letter.

invite (p. 6) – to ask someone to do something or go somewhere with you.

meal (p. 15) – the portion of food eaten at breakfast, lunch, or dinner.

meaning (pp. 4, 5) – the idea or sense of something said or written.

noun (p. 15) – a word that is the name of a person, place, or thing.

opposite (pp. 11, 13) – being completely different from another thing.

style (p. 17) – the way something is done or planned.